THE
PRINCE

THE
PRINCE

by Niccolò Machiavelli

*History's Greatest Guide to
Attaining and Keeping Power—
Now In a Special Condensation*

Abridged and Introduced
by Mitch Horowitz

THE CONDENSED 📖™ CLASSICS LIBRARY™

MEDIA

Published by Gildan Media LLC
aka G&D Media.
www.GandDmedia.com

The Prince was first printed in 1532
The Harvard Classics translation by N.H. Thomson published
1910
G&D Media Condensed Classics edition published 2019
Abridgement and Introduction copyright © 2019 by Mitch
Horowitz

FIRST PRINT AND EBOOK EDITION: 2019

Cover design by David Rheinhardt of Pyrographx

Interior design by Meghan Day Healey of Story Horse, LLC.

ISBN: 978-1-7225-0025-2

Contents

A Different Side of *The Prince*

I t does not come naturally to me to introduce and abridge Niccolò Machiavelli's 1532 classic *The Prince*. The Renaissance-era guide to gaining and holding power has been known for centuries as a blueprint to ruthlessness, deception, and even brutality. I have inveighed against current books, like *The 48 Laws of Power*, that endorse amoral or unethical methods of personal advancement.

"But that's the real world," argue the defenders of such books. Not my world. And not the one I encourage others to dwell in.

How, then, do I justify this condensed and reader-friendly new edition of *The Prince*, a book considered the urtext of guides to ruthless attainment? The fact is—as you will discover in this careful abridgement—the writer and diplomat Machiavelli imbued his work with a greater sense of purpose and ethics than is com-

monly understood. Although Machiavelli unquestion-
ably endorses absolutist and, at times, bloody ways of
dealing with adversaries, he repeatedly notes that these
are efforts of a last or near-last resort, when peace-
able means of governance prove either unpromising
or unworkable. He justifies resorting to deception or
faithlessness only as a defense against the depravity of
men, who shift alliances like the winds. This logic by
no means approaches the morality of Christ's principle
to be "wise as serpents and harmless as doves," but it
belies the general notion that Machiavelli was a one-
dimensional schemer.

Moreover, the author also emphasizes rewarding
merit; leaving the public to its own devices and personal pursuits as much as possible (which is the essential
ingredient to developing culture and economy); trusting subjects enough to allow them to bear arms—and
even to arm them yourself if confident in their loyalty
(which the good leader should be); surrounding oneself
with wise counselors (the true measure of an able ruler);
avoiding and not exploiting civic divisions; and striving
to ensure the public's general satisfaction.

One of the most striking parts of the book for me is
when Machiavelli expounds on the best kind of intellect
for an adviser or minister. In chapter XVII he writes:

> *There are three scales of intelligence, one which understands by itself, a second which understands what it is shown by others, and a third, which understands neither by itself nor by the showing of others, the first of which is most excellent, the second good, but the third worthless.*

This has always been my favorite passage of Machiavelli's. To add a further dimension to his observation, here is an alternate translation (and I challenge you to consider what place you have earned on its scale):

> *There exist three kinds of intellects: that belonging to the one who can do the thing itself, that belonging to the one who can judge the thing, and that belonging to the one who can neither do nor judge. The first is excellent, the second is good, and the third is worthless.*

Some contemporary critics suggest that *The Prince* is actually a satire of monarchy: that under the guise of a guide to ruthless conduct Machiavelli sends up the actions of absolute rulers and covertly calls for more republican forms of government. I think this assessment probably stretches matters. But it would be equally wrong, as noted, to conclude that Machiavelli was a narrow-eyed courtier bent on keeping others down. On balance, Machiavelli was a pragmatic tutor interested in promoting the unity, stability, and integrity of nation states, chiefly his own Italy, in a Europe that lacked cohesive civics and reliable international treaties. His harsher ideas were then considered acceptable quivers in the bow of statecraft; you will also see his efforts to leaven them with keen observations about the vicissitudes of human nature, fate, and virtue.

In actuality, I believe that businesspeople, leaders, and entrepreneurs who read *The Prince* today will discover subtleties that are missing from current power-at-any-cost guides. I advise experiencing *The Prince* through the filter of your own ethical standards and inner truths; sifting among its practical lessons; taking in its tough observations about human weaknesses; and using it as a guide to the realities —and foibles—of how we live.

Let me say a brief word about my method of abridgment. First, I have used the 1910 translation of Renaissance scholar N.H. Thomson, which originally appeared as part of the Harvard Classics line. My aim in condensing Thomson's translation is to provide the full range of Machiavelli's lessons and observations, but without most of his historical portraiture (which is well worth reading in the original, if you are engaged by what you encounter here). I have taken Machiavelli's most relatable and practical passages and ordered them into individual segments, each with a new and clarifying title. I have striven to eliminate repetition. I have occasionally substituted modern terms for antiquated ones. Finally, I have included a closing section of Machiavelli's most poignant aphorisms.

—Mitch Horowitz

To the Reader

I have found among my possessions none that I prize and esteem more than a knowledge of the actions of great men, acquired in the course of long experience in modern affairs and a continual study of antiquity. This knowledge has been most carefully and patiently pondered over and sifted by me, and now reduced into this little book. I can offer no better gift than the means of mastering, in a very brief time, all that in the course of so many years, and at the cost of so many hardships and dangers, I have learned, and know.

—Niccolò Machiavelli

CHAPTER I

On Acquiring a New Kingdom

The Prince cannot avoid giving offense to new subjects, either in respect of the troops he quarters on them, or of some other of the numberless vexations attendant on a new acquisition. And in this way you may find that you have enemies in all those whom you have injured in seizing the Princedom, yet cannot keep the friendship of those who helped you to gain it; since you can neither reward them as they expect, nor yet, being under obligations to them, use violent remedies against them. For however strong you may be in respect of your army, it is essential that in entering a new Province you should have the good will of its inhabitants.

Hence it happened that Louis XII of France speedily gained possession of Milan, and as speedily lost it. For the very people who had opened the gates to the French King, when they found themselves deceived in their expectations and hopes of future benefits, could not put up with the insolence of their new ruler.

True it is that when a State rebels and is again got under, it will not afterwards be lost so easily. For the Prince, using the rebellion as a pretext, will not hesitate to secure himself by punishing the guilty, bringing the suspected to trial, and otherwise strengthening his position in the points where it was weak.

I say, then, that those States which upon their acquisition are joined onto the ancient dominions of the Prince who acquires them are either of the same religion and language as the people of these dominions, or they are not. When they are, there is great ease in retaining them, especially when they have not been accustomed to live in freedom. To hold them securely it is enough to have rooted out the line of the reigning Prince; because if in other respects the old condition of things be continued, and there be no discordance in their customs, men live peaceably with one another. Even if there be some slight difference in their languages, provided that customs are similar, they can easily get on together. He, therefore, who acquires such a State, if he mean to keep it, must see to two things: first, that the blood of the ancient line of Princes be destroyed; second, that no change be made in respect of laws or taxes; for in this way the newly acquired State speedily becomes incorporated.

But when States are acquired in a country differing in language, usages, and laws, difficulties multiply, and great good fortune, as well as actions, are needed to overcome them. One of the best and most efficacious methods for dealing with such a State is for the Prince who acquires it to go and dwell there in person, since this will tend to make his tenure more secure and lasting. For when you are on the spot, disorders are detected in their beginnings and remedies can be readily applied; but when you are at a distance, they are not heard of until they have gathered strength and the case is past cure. Moreover, the Province in which you take up your abode is not pillaged by your officers; the people are pleased to have a ready recourse to their Prince; and have all the more reason if they are well disposed, to love, if disaffected, to fear him. A foreign enemy desiring to attack that State would be cautious how he did so. In short, where the Prince resides in person, it will be extremely difficult to oust him.

Another excellent expedient is to send colonies into one or two places, so that these may become, as it were, the keys of the Province; for you must either do this, or else keep up a numerous force of men-at-arms and foot soldiers. A Prince need not spend much on colonies. He can send them out and support them at little or no charge to himself, and the only persons to whom he gives offence are those whom he deprives of their fields and houses to bestow them on the new inhabitants. Those who are thus injured form but a small part of the community, and remaining scattered and poor can never become dangerous. All others being left unmolested, are in consequence easily quieted, and at the same time are afraid to make a false move, lest they share the fate of those who have been deprived of their possessions. In few words, these colonies cost less than soldiers, are more faithful, and give less offense, while those who are offended, being, as I have said, poor and dispersed, cannot hurt. And let it here be noted that men are either to be kindly treated, or utterly crushed, since they can revenge lighter injuries, but not graver. Wherefore the injury we do to a man should be of a sort to leave no fear of reprisals.

Chapter II

Against Occupation

If instead of colonies you send troops, the cost is vastly greater, and the whole revenues of the country are spent in guarding it; so that the gain becomes a loss, and much deeper offense is given; since in shifting the quarters of your soldiers from place to place the whole country suffers hardship, which as all feel, all are made enemies; and enemies who remaining, although vanquished, in their own homes, have power to hurt. In every way, therefore, this mode of defense is as disadvantageous as that by colonizing is useful.

In dealing with the countries of which they took possession the Romans diligently followed the methods I have described. They planted colonies, conciliated weaker powers without adding to their strength, humbled the great, and never suffered a formidable stranger to acquire influence.

Chapter III

The Example of
Alexander the Great

Alexander the Great having achieved the conquest of Asia in a few years and, dying before he had well entered on possession, it might have been expected, given the difficulty of preserving newly acquired States, that on his death the whole country would rise in revolt.

Nevertheless, his successors were able to keep their hold, and found in doing so no other difficulty than arose from their own ambition and mutual jealousies.

If anyone think this strange and ask the cause, I answer that all the Princedoms of which we have record have been governed in one of two ways: 1) either by a sole Prince, all others being his servants permitted by his grace and favor to assist in governing the kingdom as his ministers; or 2) by a Prince with his Barons who hold their rank, not by the favor of a superior Lord, but by antiquity of bloodline, and who have States and subjects of their own who recognize them as their rulers and entertain for them a natural affection.

States governed by a sole Prince and by his servants—as with Alexander—vest in him a more complete authority; because throughout the land none but he is recognized as sovereign, and if obedience be yielded to any others, it is yielded as to his ministers and officers for whom personally no special love is felt.*

---

* Machiavelli is saying that civic and military authority surpasses bloodline.—MH

Chapter IV

How to Control Formerly Independent Territories

When a newly acquired State has been accustomed to live under its own laws and in freedom, there are three methods whereby it may be held. The first is to destroy it; the second, to go and reside there in person; the third, to suffer it to live on under its own laws, subjecting it to a tribute and entrusting its government to a few of the inhabitants who will keep the rest your friends. Such a Government, since it is the creature of the new Prince, will see that it cannot stand without his protection and support, and must therefore do all it can to maintain him; and a city accustomed to live in freedom, if it is to be preserved at all, is more easily controlled through its own citizens than in any other way.

We have examples of all these methods in the histories of the Spartans and the Romans. The Spartans held Athens and Thebes by creating oligarchies in these cities, yet lost them in the end. The Romans, to retain Capua, Carthage, and Numantia, destroyed them and never lost them. On the other hand, when they thought to hold Greece as the Spartans had held it, leaving it its freedom and allowing it to be governed by its own laws, they failed, and had to destroy many cities of that Province before they could secure it. For, in truth, there is no sure way of holding other than by destroying, and whoever becomes master of a City accustomed to live in freedom and does not destroy it, may reckon on being destroyed by it. For if it should rebel, it can always screen itself under the name of liberty and its ancient laws, which no length of time, nor any benefits conferred will ever cause it to forget; and do what you will, and take what care you may, unless the inhabitants be scattered and dispersed, this name, and the old order of things, will never cease to be remembered, but will at once be turned against you whenever misfortune overtakes you.

If, however, the newly acquired City or Province has been accustomed to live under a Prince, and his line is extinguished, it will be impossible for the citizens, used, on the one hand, to obey, and deprived, on the other, of their old ruler, to agree to choose a leader from among themselves; and as they know not how to live as freemen, and are therefore slow to take up arms, a stranger may readily gain them over and attach them to his cause. But in Republics there is a stronger vitality, a fiercer hatred, a keener thirst for revenge. The memory of their former freedom will not let them rest; so that the safest course is either to destroy them, or to go and live in them.

CHAPTER V

When a Prince Conquers by Merit

Since men for the most part follow in the footsteps and imitate the actions of others, and yet are unable to adhere exactly to those paths which others have taken, or attain to the virtues of those whom they would resemble, the wise man should always follow the roads that have been trodden by the great, and imitate those who have most excelled, so that if he cannot reach their perfection, he may at least acquire something of its savor. Acting in this like the skillful archer, who seeing that the object he would hit is distant, and knowing the range of his bow, takes aim much above the destined mark; not designing that his arrow should strike so high, but that flying high it may strike the point intended.

I say, then, that in entirely new Princedoms where the Prince himself is new, the difficulty of maintaining possession varies with the greater or less ability of him who acquires possession. And, because the mere fact of a private person rising to be a Prince presupposes either merit or good fortune, it will be seen that the presence of one or other of these two conditions lessens, to some extent, many difficulties. And yet, he who is less beholden to Fortune has often in the end the better success; and it may be for the advantage of a Prince that, from his having no other territories, he is obliged to reside in person in the State which he has acquired.

Looking first to those who have become Princes by their merit and not by their good fortune, I say that the most excellent among them are Moses, Cyrus, Romulus, Theseus, and the like. And though perhaps I ought not to name Moses, he being merely an instrument for carrying out the Divine commands, he is still to be admired for those qualities which made him worthy to converse with God. But if we consider Cyrus and the others who have acquired or founded kingdoms, they will all be seen to be admirable. And if their actions and the particular institutions of which they were the authors be studied, they will be found not to differ from those of Moses, instructed though he was by so great a teacher. Moreover, on examining their lives and actions, we shall see that they were debtors to Fortune for nothing beyond the opportunity which enabled them to shape things as they pleased, without which the force of their spirit would have been spent in vain; as on the other hand, opportunity would have offered itself in vain had the capacity for turning it to account been wanting. It was necessary, therefore, that Moses should find the children of Israel in bondage in Egypt, and oppressed by the Egyptians, in order that they might be disposed to follow him, and so escape from their servitude. It was fortunate for Romulus that he found no home in Alba, but was exposed at the time of his birth, to the end that he might become king and founder of the City of Rome. It was necessary that Cyrus should find the Persians discontented with the rule of the Medes, and the Medes enervated and effeminate from a prolonged peace. Nor could Theseus have displayed his great qualities had he not found the Athenians disunited and dispersed. But while it was their opportunities that made these men fortunate, it was their own merit that enabled them to recognize these opportunities and turn them to account, to the glory and prosperity of their country.

They who come to the Princedom, as these did, by virtuous paths, acquire with difficulty, but keep with ease. The difficulties which they have in acquiring arise mainly from the new laws and institutions that they are forced to introduce in founding and securing their government. And let it be noted that there is no more delicate matter to take in hand, nor more dangerous to conduct, nor more doubtful in its success, than to set up as a leader in the introduction of changes. For he who innovates will have for his enemies all those who are well off under the existing order of things, and only lukewarm supporters in those who might be better off under the new. This lukewarm temper arises partly from the fear of adversaries who have the laws on their side, and partly from the incredulity of mankind, who will never admit the merit of anything new, until they have seen it proved by the event. The result, however, is that whenever the enemies of change make an attack, they do so with all the zeal of partisans, while the others defend themselves so feebly as to endanger both themselves and their cause.

It should be borne in mind that the temper of the multitude is fickle, and that while it is easy to persuade them of a thing, it is hard to fix them in that persuasion. Wherefore, matters should be so ordered that when men no longer believe of their own accord, they may be compelled to believe by force. Moses, Cyrus, Theseus, and Romulus could never have made their ordinances be observed for any length of time had they been unarmed, as was the case, in our own days, with the Friar Girolamo Savonarola, whose new institutions came to nothing so soon as the multitude began to waver in their faith; since he had not the means to keep those who had been believers steadfast in their belief, or to make unbelievers believe.

Such persons, therefore, have great difficulty in carrying out their designs; but all their difficulties are on the road, and may be overcome by courage. Having conquered these, and coming to be held in reverence, and having destroyed all who were jealous of their influence, they remain powerful, safe, honored, and prosperous.

CHAPTER VI

When a Prince Conquers with Help of Others or by Luck

They who from private life become Princes by mere good fortune, do so with little trouble, but have much trouble to maintain themselves. They meet with no hindrance on their way, being carried as it were on wings to their destination, but all their difficulties overtake them when they alight. Of this class are those on whom States are conferred either in return for money, or through the favor of him who confers them.

Such Princes are wholly dependent on the favor and fortunes of those who have made them great; of supports none could be less stable or secure; and they lack both the knowledge and the power that would enable them to maintain their position. They lack the knowledge because, unless they have great parts and force of character, it is not to be expected that having always lived in a private station they should have learned how to command. They lack the power since they cannot look for support from attached and faithful troops. Moreover, States suddenly acquired, like all else that is produced and grows up rapidly, can never have such root or hold as that the first storm which strikes them shall not overthrow them; unless, indeed that they who suddenly become Princes have a capacity for learning quickly how to defend what Fortune has placed in their lap, and can lay those foundations after they rise which by others are laid before.

He who does not lay his foundations at first, may, if he be of great ability, succeed in laying them afterwards, though with inconvenience to the builder and risk to the building.

A certain type of man will judge it necessary, on entering a new Princedom, to rid himself of enemies, to conciliate friends, to prevail by force or fraud, to make himself feared yet not hated by his subjects, respected and obeyed by his soldiers, to crush those who can or ought to injure him, to introduce changes in the old order of things, to be at once severe and affable, magnanimous and liberal, to do away with a mutinous army and create a new one, to maintain relations with Kings and Princes on such a footing that they must see it for their interest to aid him, and dangerous to offend.

CHAPTER VII

When a Prince
Conquers by Crime

A man may also rise from privacy to be a Prince in one of two ways, neither of which can be ascribed wholly either to merit or to fortune. The ways I speak of are, first, when the ascent to power is made by paths of wickedness and crime; and, second, when a private person becomes ruler of his country by the favor of his fellow-citizens.

Whoever examines the first man's actions and achievements will discover little or nothing in them which can be ascribed to Fortune, seeing that it was not through the favor of any but by the regular steps of the military service, gained at the cost of a thousand hardships and hazards, he reached the princedom, which he afterwards maintained by so many daring and dangerous enterprises. Still, to slaughter fellow-citizens, to betray friends, to be devoid of honor, pity, and religion, cannot be counted as merits, for these are means which may lead to power, but which confer no glory.

On seizing a state, the usurper should make haste to inflict what injuries he must, at a stroke, that he may not have to renew them daily, but be enabled by their discontinuance to reassure men's minds and afterwards win them over by benefits. Whosoever, either through timidity or from following bad counsels adopts a contrary course must keep the sword always drawn, and can put no trust in his subjects, who suffering from continued and constantly renewed severities, will never yield him their confidence. Injuries, therefore, should be inflicted all at once that their ill savor being less lasting may the less offend; whereas, benefits should be conferred little by little that so they may be more fully relished.

But, above all things, a Prince should so live with his subjects that no vicissitude of good or evil fortune shall oblige him to alter his behavior; because, if a need to change should come through adversity, it is then too late to resort to severity; while any leniency that you may use will be thrown away, for it will be seen to be compulsory and gain you no thanks.

CHAPTER VIII

When a Prince Rules by Popular Consent

I come now to the second case, namely, of the leading citizen who, not by crimes or violence, but by the favor of his fellow-citizens is made Prince of his country. This may be called a Civil Princedom, and its attainment depends not wholly on merit, nor wholly on good fortune, but rather on what may be termed a fortunate astuteness. I say then that the road to this Princedom lies either through the favor of the people or of the nobles. For in every city are to be found these two opposed humors having their origin in this: that the people desire not to be domineered over or oppressed by the nobles, while the nobles desire to oppress and domineer over the people. And from these two contrary appetites there arises in cities one of three results: a Princedom, or Liberty, or License. A Princedom is created either by the people or by the nobles, according as one or other of these factions has occasion for it. For when the nobles perceive that they cannot withstand the people, they set to work to magnify the reputation of one of their number, and make him their Prince, to the end that under his shadow they may be enabled to indulge their desires. The people, on the other hand, when they see that they cannot make head against the nobles, invest a single citizen with all their influence and make him Prince, that they may have the shelter of his authority.

He who is made Prince by the favor of the nobles, has greater difficulty to maintain himself than he who comes to the Princedom by aid of the people, since he finds many about him who think themselves as good as he, and whom, on that account, he cannot guide or govern as he would. But he who reaches the Princedom by the popular support, finds himself alone, with none, or but a very few about him who are not ready to obey. Moreover, the demands of the nobles cannot be satisfied with credit to the Prince, nor without injury to others, while those of the people well may, the aim of the people being more honorable than that of the nobles, the latter seeking to oppress, the former not to be oppressed. Add to this, that a Prince can never secure himself against a disaffected people, their number being too great, while he may against a disaffected nobility, since their number is small. The worst that a Prince need fear from a disaffected people is that they may desert him, whereas when the nobles are his enemies he has to fear not only that they may desert him but also that they may turn against him; because, as they have greater craft and foresight, they always choose their time to suit their safety, and seek favor with the side they think will win. Again, a Prince must always live with the same people but need not always live with the same nobles, being able to make and unmake these from day to day, and give and take away their authority at his pleasure.

But to make this part of the matter clearer, I say that as regards the nobles there is this first distinction to be made. They either so govern their conduct as to bind themselves wholly to your fortunes, or they do not. Those who so bind themselves, and who are not grasping, should be loved and honored. As to those who do not so bind themselves, there is this further distinction. For the most part they are held back by pusillanimity and a natural defect of courage, in which case you should make use of them, and of those among them more especially who are prudent, for they will do you honor in prosperity, and in adversity give you no cause for fear. But where they abstain from attaching themselves to you of set purpose and for ambitious ends, it is a sign that they are thinking more of themselves than of you, and against such men a Prince should be on his guard, and treat them as though they were declared enemies, for in his adversity they will always help to ruin him.

He who becomes a Prince through the favor of the people should always keep on good terms with them; which it is easy for him to do, since all they ask is not to be oppressed. But he who against the will of the people is made a Prince by the favor of the nobles, must, above all things, seek to conciliate the people, which he readily may by taking them under his protection. For since men who are well treated by one whom they expected to treat them ill feel the more beholden to their benefactor, the people will at once become better disposed to such a Prince when he protects them than if he owed his Princedom to them.

There are many ways in which a Prince may gain the goodwill of the people, but, because these vary with circumstances, no certain rule can be laid down respecting them, and I shall, therefore, say no more about them. But this is the sum of the matter, that it is essential for a Prince to be on a friendly footing with his people since otherwise he will have no resource in adversity.

And what I affirm let no one controvert by citing the old saw that 'he who builds on the people builds on mire,' for that may be true of a private citizen who presumes on his favor with the people, and counts on being rescued by them when overpowered by his enemies or by the magistrates. In such cases a man may often find himself deceived. But when he who builds on the people is a Prince capable of command, of a spirit not to be cast down by ill-fortune, who, while he animates the whole community by his courage and bearing, neglects no prudent precaution, he will not find himself betrayed by the people, but will be seen to have laid his foundations well.

The most critical juncture for Princedoms of this kind, is at the moment when they are about to pass from the popular to the absolute form of government: and as these Princes exercise their authority either directly or through the agency of the magistrates, in the latter case their position is weaker and more hazardous, since they are wholly in the power of those citizens to whom the magistracies are entrusted, who can, and especially in difficult times with the greatest ease, deprive them of their authority, either by opposing or by not obeying them. And in times of peril it is too late for a Prince to assume to himself an absolute authority, for the citizens and subjects who are accustomed to take their orders from the magistrates will not when dangers threaten take them from the Prince, so that at such seasons there will always be very few in whom he can trust. Such Princes, therefore, must not build on what they see in tranquil times when the citizens feel the need of the State. For then everyone is ready to run, to promise, and, danger of death being remote, even to die for the State. But in troubled times, when the State has need of its citizens, few of them are to be found. And the risk of the experiment is the greater in that it can only be made once. Wherefore, a wise Prince should devise means whereby his subjects may at all times, whether favorable or adverse, feel the need of the State and of him, and then they will always be faithful to him.

Chapter IX

How the Strength of Princedoms Should Be Measured

In examining the character of these Princedoms, another circumstance has to be considered, namely, whether the Prince is strong enough, if occasion demands, to stand alone, or whether he needs continual help from others. To make the matter clearer, I pronounce those to be able to stand alone who, with the men and money at their disposal, can get together an army fit to take the field against any assailant; and, conversely, I judge those to be in constant need of help who cannot take the field against their enemies, but are obliged to retire behind their walls, and to defend themselves there. As to the latter there is nothing to be said, except to exhort such Princes to strengthen and fortify the towns in which they dwell, and take no heed of the country outside. For whoever has thoroughly fortified his town, and put himself on such a footing with his subjects as I have already indicated and shall further speak of, will always be attacked with much caution; for men are always averse to enterprises that are attended with difficulty, and it is impossible not to foresee difficulties in attacking a Prince whose town is strongly fortified and who is not hated by his subjects.

A Prince, therefore, who has a strong city, and who does not make himself hated, cannot be attacked, or should he be so, his assailant will come badly off, since human affairs are so variable that it is almost impossible for anyone to keep an army posted for a whole year without interruption of some sort. Should it be objected that if the citizens have possessions outside the town and see them burned they will lose patience, and that self-interest, together with the hardships of a protracted siege, will cause them to forget their loyalty, I answer that a capable and courageous Prince will always overcome these difficulties by holding out hopes to his subjects that the evil will not be of long continuance; by exciting their fears of the enemy's cruelty; and by dexterously silencing those who seem to him too forward in their complaints. Moreover, it is to be expected that the enemy will burn and lay waste the country immediately on their arrival, at a time when men's minds are still heated and resolute for defense. And for this very reason the Prince has less to fear because after a few days, when the first ardor has abated, the injury is already done and suffered and cannot be undone; and the people will now, all the more readily, make common cause with their Prince from his seeming to be under obligations to them, their houses having been burned and their lands wasted in his defense. For it is the nature of men to incur obligation as much by the benefits they render as by those they receive.

If the whole matter be well considered, it ought not to be difficult for a prudent Prince, both at the outset and afterwards, to maintain the spirits of his subjects during a siege; provided always that provisions and other means of defense do not run short.

Chapter X

Of Soldiers and Mercenaries

The arms with which a Prince defends his State are either his own subjects, or they are mercenaries, or they are auxiliaries, or they are partly one and partly another. Mercenaries and auxiliaries are at once useless and dangerous, and he who holds his State by means of mercenary troops can never be solidly or securely seated. For such troops are disunited, ambitious, insubordinate, treacherous, insolent among friends, cowardly before foes, and without fear of God or faith with man. Whenever they are attacked defeat follows; so that in peace you are plundered by them, in war by your enemies. And this is because they have no tie or motive to keep them in the field beyond their paltry pay, in return for which it would be too much to expect them to give their lives. They are ready enough, therefore, to be your soldiers while you are at peace, but when war is declared they make off and disappear.

I ought to have little difficulty in getting this believed, for the present ruin of Italy is due to no other cause than her having for many years trusted to mercenaries, who though heretofore they may have helped the fortunes of some one man, and made a show of strength when matched with one another, have always revealed themselves in their true colors so soon as foreign enemies appeared.

The second sort of unprofitable arms are auxiliaries, by whom I mean troops brought to help and protect you by a potentate whom you summon to your aid; as when in recent times, Pope Julius II, observing the pitiful behavior of his mercenaries at the enterprise of Ferrara, betook himself to auxiliaries, and arranged with Ferdinand of Spain to be supplied with horse and foot soldiers.*

Auxiliaries may be excellent and useful soldiers for themselves, but are always hurtful to him who calls them in; for if they are defeated, he is undone; if victorious, he becomes their prisoner. Ancient histories abound with instances of this.

Let him, therefore, who would deprive himself of every chance of success, have recourse to auxilia-

---

* Julius was later forced to make territorial concessions to Ferdinand. —MH

ries, these being far more dangerous than mercenary arms, bringing ruin with them ready made. For they are united, and wholly under the control of their own officers; whereas, before mercenaries, even after gaining a victory, can do you hurt, longer time and better opportunities are needed; because, as they are made up of separate companies, raised and paid by you, he whom you place in command cannot at once acquire such authority over them as will be injurious to you. In short, with mercenaries your greatest danger is from their inertness and cowardice, with auxiliaries from their valor. Wise Princes, therefore, have always eschewed these arms, and trusted rather to their own, and have preferred defeat with the latter to victory with the former, counting that as no true victory which is gained by foreign aid.

Chapter XI

The Prince and Military Affairs

A Prince, therefore, should have no care or thought other than for war, and for the regulations and training it requires, and should apply himself exclusively to this as his peculiar province; for war is the sole art looked for in one who rules, and is of such efficacy that it not merely maintains those who are born Princes, but often enables men to rise to that eminence from a private station; while, on the other hand, we often see that when Princes devote themselves rather to pleasure than to arms, they lose their dominions. And as neglect of this art is the prime cause of such calamities, to be proficient in it is the surest way to acquire power.

Between an armed and an unarmed man no proportion holds, and it is contrary to reason to expect that the armed man should voluntarily submit to him who is unarmed, or that the unarmed man should stand secure among armed retainers. For with contempt on one side and distrust on the other it is impossible that men should work well together. Wherefore, as has already been said, a Prince who is ignorant of military affairs, besides other disadvantages, can neither be respected by his soldiers, nor can he trust them. A Prince, therefore, ought never to allow his attention to be diverted from warlike pursuits, and should occupy himself with them even more in peace than in war. This he can do in two ways, by practice or by study.

As to the practice, he ought, besides keeping his soldiers well trained and disciplined, to be constantly engaged in the chase, that he may inure his body to hardships and fatigue, and gain at the same time a knowledge of places, by observing how the mountains slope, the valleys open, and the plains spread; acquainting himself with the characters of rivers and marshes, and giving the greatest attention to this subject. Such knowledge is useful to him in two ways; for first, he learns thereby to know his own country, and to understand better how it may be defended; and next, from his familiar acquaintance with its localities, he readily comprehends the character of other districts when obliged to observe them for the first time. For the hills, valleys, plains, rivers, and marshes of Tuscany, for example, have a certain resemblance to those elsewhere;

so that from a knowledge of the natural features of that province, similar knowledge in respect of other provinces may readily be gained. The Prince who is wanting in this kind of knowledge, is wanting in the first qualification of a good captain for by it he is taught how to surprise an enemy, how to choose an encampment, how to lead his army on a march, how to array it for battle, and how to post it to the best advantage for a siege.

Among the commendations that Philopoemen, Prince of the Achaeans, has received from historians is this: that in times of peace he was always thinking of methods of warfare, so that when walking in the country with his friends he would often stop and talk with them on the subject. "If the enemy," he would say, "were posted on that hill, and we found ourselves here with our army, which of us would have the better position? How could we most safely and in the best order advance to meet them? If we had to retreat, what direction should we take? If they retired, how should we pursue?" In this way he put to his friends, as he went along, all the contingencies that can befall an army. He listened to their opinions, stated his own, and supported them with reasons; and from his being constantly occupied with such meditations, it resulted, that when in actual command no complication could ever present itself with which he was not prepared to deal.

As to the mental training of which we have spoken, a Prince should read histories, and in these should note the actions of great men, observe how they conducted themselves in their wars, and examine the causes of their victories and defeats. And above all, he should, as many great men of past ages have done, assume for his models those persons who before his time have been renowned and celebrated, whose deeds and achievements he should constantly keep in mind.

A wise Prince, therefore, should pursue such methods as these, never resting idle in times of peace but strenuously seeking to turn them to account, so that he may derive strength from them in the hour of danger, and find himself ready should Fortune turn against him.

CHAPTER XII

Better to Be Loved or Feared?

I say that every Prince should desire to be accounted merciful and not cruel. Nevertheless, he should be on his guard against the abuse of this quality of mercy.

A Prince should disregard the reproach of being thought cruel where it enables him to keep his subjects united and obedient. For he who quells disorder by a very few signal examples will in the end be more merciful than he who from too great leniency permits things to take their course and so to result in pillage and bloodshed; for these hurt the whole State, whereas the severities of the Prince injure individuals only. And for a new Prince, of all others, it is impossible to escape a name for cruelty, since new States are full of dangers.

Nevertheless, the new Prince should not be too ready of belief, nor too easily set in motion; nor should he himself be the first to raise alarms; but should so temper prudence with kindliness that too great confidence in others shall not throw him off his guard nor groundless distrust render him insupportable.

And here comes in the question whether it is better to be loved rather than feared, or feared rather than loved. It might perhaps be answered that we should wish to be both; but since love and fear can hardly exist together, if we must choose between them, it is far safer to be feared than loved. For of men it may generally be affirmed that they are thankless, fickle, false, studious to avoid danger, greedy of gain, devoted to you while you are able to confer benefits upon them, and ready, as I said before, while danger is distant, to shed their blood, and sacrifice their property, their lives, and their children for you; but in the hour of need they turn against you. The Prince, therefore, who without otherwise securing himself builds wholly on their professions is undone. For the friendships which we buy with a price, and do not gain by greatness and nobility of character, though they be fairly earned are not made good, but fail us when we have occasion to use them.

Moreover, men are less careful how they offend him who makes himself loved than him who makes himself feared. For love is held by the tie of obligation, which, because men are a sorry breed, is broken on every whisper of private interest; but fear is bound by the apprehension of punishment which never relaxes its grasp.

Nevertheless a Prince should inspire fear in such a fashion that if he do not win love he may escape hate. For a man may very well be feared and yet not hated, and this will be the case so long as he does not meddle with the property or with the women of his citizens and subjects. And if constrained to put any to death, he should do so only when there is manifest cause or reasonable justification. But, above all, he must abstain from seizing the property of others. For men will sooner forget the death of their father than the loss of their estate. Moreover, pretexts for confiscation are difficult to find, and he who has once begun to live by pillaging always finds reasons for taking what is not his; whereas reasons for shedding blood are fewer and sooner exhausted.

Among other things remarkable in Hannibal, this has been noted: that having a very great army, made up of men of many different nations and brought to fight in a foreign country, no dissension ever arose among the soldiers themselves, nor any mutiny against their leader, either in his good or in his evil fortunes. This we can only ascribe to the transcendent cruelty, which, joined with numberless great qualities, rendered him at once venerable and terrible in the eyes of his soldiers, for without this reputation for cruelty these other virtues would not have produced the like results.

CHAPTER XIII

Truth and Deception

Everyone understands how praiseworthy it is in a Prince to maintain trust, and to live uprightly and not craftily. Nevertheless, we see from what has taken place in our own days that Princes who have set little store by their word, but have known how to overreach men by their cunning, have accomplished great things, and in the end got the better of those who trusted to honest dealing.

Be it known, then, that there are two ways of contending, one in accordance with the laws, the other by force; the first of which is proper to men, the second to beasts. But since the first method is often ineffectual, it becomes necessary to resort to the second. A Prince should, therefore, understand how to use well both the man and the beast. And this lesson has been covertly taught by the ancient writers who relate how Achilles and many others of these old Princes were given over to be brought up and trained by Chiron the Centaur; the only meaning of their having for an instructor one who was half man and half beast is that it is necessary for a Prince to know how to use both natures, and that the one without the other has no stability.

But since a Prince should know how to use the beast's nature wisely, he ought of beasts to choose both the lion and the fox; for the lion cannot guard himself from the traps nor the fox from wolves. He must therefore be a fox to discern traps and a lion to drive off wolves.

To rely wholly on the lion is unwise; and for this reason a prudent Prince neither can nor ought to keep his word when to keep it is hurtful to him, and the causes which led him to pledge it are removed. If all men were good this would not be good advice, but since they are dishonest and do not keep faith with you, you in return need not keep faith with them; and no prince was ever at a loss for plausible reasons to cloak a breach of faith. Of this numberless recent instances could be given, and it might be shown how many solemn treaties and engagements have been rendered inoperative and idle through want of faith in Princes, and that he who was best known to play the fox has had the best success.

It is necessary, indeed, to put a good color on this nature, and to be skillful in simulating and dissembling.

But men are so simple, and governed so absolutely by their present needs, that he who wishes to deceive will never fail in finding willing dupes.

And you are to understand that a Prince, and most of all a new Prince, cannot observe all those rules of conduct in respect whereof men are accounted good, being often forced, in order to preserve his Princedom, to act in opposition to good faith, charity, humanity, and religion. He must therefore keep his mind ready to shift as the winds and tides of Fortune turn, and, as I have already said, he ought not to quit good courses if he can help it, but should know how to follow evil courses if he must.

A Prince should therefore be very careful that nothing ever escapes his lips that does not make him seem the embodiment of mercy, good faith, integrity, humanity, and religion. And there is no virtue which it is more necessary for him to seem to possess than this last; because men in general judge rather by the eye than by the hand, for everyone can see but few can touch. Everyone sees what you seem, but few know what you are, and these few dare not oppose themselves to the opinion of the many who have the majesty of the State to back them up.

Moreover, in the actions of all men, and most of all of Princes, where there is no tribunal to which we can appeal we look to results. Wherefore if a Prince succeeds in establishing and maintaining his authority the means will always be judged honorable and be approved by everyone. For the vulgar are always taken by appearances and by results, and the world is made up of the vulgar, the few only finding room when the many have no longer ground to stand on.

A certain Prince of our own days, whose name it is as well not to mention, is always preaching peace and good faith, although the mortal enemy of both; and both, had he practiced them as he preaches them, would, oftener than once, have lost him his kingdom and authority.

Chapter XIV

How to Avert Conspiracies

A Prince should consider how he may avoid such courses as would make him hated or despised; and that whenever he succeeds in keeping clear of these, he has performed his part, and runs no risk though he incur other infamies.

A Prince, as I have said before, sooner becomes hated by being rapacious and by interfering with the property and with the women of his subjects than in any other way. From these, therefore, he should abstain. For so long as neither their property nor their honor are touched the mass of mankind live contentedly, and the Prince has only to cope with the ambition of a few, which can in many ways and easily be kept within bounds.

A Prince is despised when he is seen to be fickle, frivolous, effeminate, pusillanimous, or irresolute, against which defects he ought therefore most carefully to guard, striving so to bear himself that greatness, courage, wisdom, and strength may appear in all his actions. In his private dealings with his subjects his decisions should be irrevocable, and his reputation such that no one would dream of overreaching or cajoling him.

The Prince who inspires such an opinion of himself is greatly esteemed, and against one who is greatly esteemed conspiracy is difficult; nor, when he is known to be an excellent Prince and held in reverence by his subjects, will it be easy to attack him. For a Prince is exposed to two dangers: from within in respect of his subjects, and from without in respect of foreign powers. Against the latter he will defend himself with good arms and good allies, and if he have good arms he will always have good allies; and when things are settled abroad, they will always be settled at home, unless disturbed by conspiracies; and even should there be hostility from without, if he has taken those measures, and has lived in the way I have recommended, and if he never abandons hope, he will withstand every attack.

As regards his own subjects, when affairs are quiet abroad, he has to fear they may engage in secret plots; against which a Prince best secures himself when he escapes being hated or despised, and keeps on good terms with his people; and this, as I have already shown, is essential. Not to be hated or despised by the body of his subjects is one of the surest safeguards that a Prince can have against conspiracy. For he who conspires always reckons on pleasing the people by putting the Prince to death; but when he sees that instead of pleasing he will offend them, he cannot summon courage to carry out his design. For the difficulties that attend conspirators are infinite, and we know from experience that while there have been many conspiracies, few of them have succeeded.

He who conspires cannot do so alone, nor can he assume as his companions any save those whom he believes to be discontented; but so soon as you impart your design to a discontented man, you supply him with the means of removing his discontent, since by betraying you he can procure for himself every advantage; so that seeing on the one hand certain gain and on the other a doubtful and dangerous risk, he must either be a rare friend to you or the mortal enemy of his Prince, if he keep your secret.

To put the matter shortly, I say that on the side of the conspirator there are distrust, jealousy, and dread of punishment to deter him; while on the side of the Prince there are the laws, the majesty of the throne, the protection of friends and of the government to defend him, to which if the general goodwill of the people be added, it is hardly possible that any should be rash enough to conspire. For while in ordinary cases, the conspirator has ground for fear only before the execution of his villainy, in this case he has also cause to fear after the crime has been perpetrated since he has the people for his enemy and is thus cut off from every hope of shelter.

In brief, a Prince has little to fear from conspiracies when his subjects are well disposed towards him; but when they are hostile and hold him in detestation he has then reason to fear everything and everyone. And well ordered States and wise Princes have provided with extreme care that the nobility shall not be driven to desperation, and that the commons shall be kept satisfied and contented; for this is one of the most important matters that a Prince must look to.

CHAPTER XV

How a Prince
Should Defend Himself

To govern more securely some Princes have disarmed their subjects, others have kept the towns subject to them divided by factions; some have fostered hostility against themselves, others have sought to gain over those who at the beginning of their reign were looked on with suspicion; some have built fortresses, others have dismantled and destroyed them; and though no definite judgment can be pronounced respecting any of these methods, without regard to the special circumstances of the State to which it is proposed to apply them, I shall nevertheless speak of them in as comprehensive a way as the subject will admit.

It has never chanced that any new Prince has disarmed his subjects. On the contrary, when he has found them unarmed he has always armed them. For the arms thus provided become yours, those whom you suspected grow faithful, while those who were faithful at the first continue so, and from your subjects become your partisans. And though all your subjects cannot be armed yet if those of them whom you arm be treated with marked favor you can deal more securely with the rest. For the difference which those whom you supply with arms perceive in their treatment will bind them to you, while the others will excuse you recognizing that those who incur greater risk and responsibility merit greater rewards. But by disarming, you at once give offense, since you show your subjects that you distrust them, either as doubting their courage or as doubting their fidelity, each of which imputations begets hatred against you. Moreover, as you cannot maintain yourself without arms you must have recourse to mercenary troops. What these are I have already shown, but even if they were good, they could never avail to defend you at once against powerful enemies abroad and against subjects whom you distrust. Wherefore, as I have said already, new Princes in new Princedoms have always provided for their being armed; and of instances of this History is full.

But when a Prince acquires a new State, which thus becomes joined on like a limb to his old possessions, he must disarm its inhabitants, except such of them as have taken part with him while he was acquiring it; and even these, as time and occasion serve, he should seek to render soft and effeminate; and he must so manage matters that all the arms of the new State shall be in the hands of his own soldiers who have served under him in his ancient dominions.

I do not believe that divisions purposely caused can ever lead to good; on the contrary, when an enemy approaches, divided cities are lost at once, for the weaker faction will always side with the invader, and the other will not be able to stand alone.

Moreover methods like these argue weakness in a Prince, for under a strong government divisions would never be permitted, since they are profitable only in time of peace as an expedient whereby subjects may be more easily managed; but when war breaks out their insufficiency is demonstrated.

It has been customary for Princes, with a view to hold their dominions more securely, to build fortresses which might serve as a curb and restraint on such as have designs against them, and as a safe refuge against a first onset. I approve this custom, because it has been followed from the earliest times.

Fortresses are useful or not according to circumstances, and if in one way they benefit, in another they injure you. We may state the case thus: the Prince who is more afraid of his subjects than of strangers ought to build fortresses, while he who is more afraid of strangers than of his subjects should leave them alone.

All considerations taken into account, I shall applaud him who builds fortresses and him who does not; but I shall blame him who, trusting in them, reckons it a light thing to be held in hatred by his people.

CHAPTER XVI

How a Prince Should Preserve His Reputation

N othing makes a Prince so well thought of as to undertake great enterprises and give striking proofs of his capacity.

It greatly profits a Prince in conducting the internal government of his State to follow striking methods. The remarkable actions of anyone in civil life, whether for good or for evil, afford him notability; and to choose such ways of rewarding and punishing cannot fail to be much spoken of. But above all, he should strive by all his actions to inspire a sense of his greatness and goodness.

A Prince is likewise esteemed who is a stanch friend and a thorough foe, that is to say, who without reserve openly declares for one against another, this being always a more advantageous course than to stand neutral. For supposing two of your powerful neighbors come to blows, it must either be that you have, or have not, reason to fear the one who comes off victorious. In either case it will always be well for you to declare yourself, and join in frankly with one side or other. For should you fail to do so you are certain, in the former of the cases put, to become the prey of the victor to the satisfaction and delight of the vanquished, and no reason or circumstance that you may plead will avail to shield or shelter you; for the victor dislikes doubtful friends, and such as will not help him at a pinch; and the vanquished will have nothing to say to you, since you would not share his fortunes sword in hand.

A Prince should be careful never to join with one stronger than himself in attacking others, unless he is driven to it by necessity. For if he whom you join prevails, you are at his mercy; and Princes, so far as in them lies, should avoid placing themselves at the mercy of others.

A Prince should show himself a patron of merit, and should honor those who excel in every art. He ought accordingly to encourage his subjects by enabling them to pursue their callings, whether mercantile, agricultural, or any other, in security, so that this man shall not be deterred from beautifying his possessions from the apprehension that they may be taken from him, or that other refrain from opening a trade through fear of taxes; and he should provide rewards for those who desire so to employ themselves, and for all who are disposed in any way to add to the greatness of his City or State.

He ought, moreover, at suitable seasons of the year to entertain the people with festivals and shows. And because all cities are divided into guilds and companies, he should show attention to these societies, and sometimes take part in their meetings, offering an example of courtesy and munificence, but always maintaining the dignity of his station, which must under no circumstances be compromised.

CHAPTER XVII

A Prince's Court

The choice of Ministers is a matter of no small moment to a Prince. Whether they shall be good or not depends on his prudence, so that the readiest conjecture we can form of the character and sagacity of a Prince is from seeing what sort of men he has about him. When they are at once capable and faithful, we may always account him wise, since he has known to recognize their merit and to retain their fidelity. But if they be otherwise, we must pronounce unfavorably of him, since he has committed a first fault in making this selection.

There are three scales of intelligence, one which understands by itself, a second which understands what it is shown by others, and a third which understands neither by itself nor by the showing of others, the first of which is most excellent, the second good, but the third worthless.

As to how a Prince is to know his Minister, this unerring rule may be laid down. When you see a Minister thinking more of himself than of you, and in all his actions seeking his own ends, that man can never be a good Minister or one that you can trust. For he who has the charge of the State committed to him, ought not to think of himself, but only of his Prince, and should never bring to the notice of the latter what does not directly concern him. On the other hand, to keep his Minister good, the Prince should be considerate of him, dignifying him, enriching him, binding him to himself by benefits, and sharing with him the honors as well as the burdens of the State, so that the abundant honors and wealth bestowed upon him may divert him from seeking them at other hands; while the great responsibilities wherewith he is charged may lead him to dread change, knowing that he cannot stand alone without his master's support. When Prince and Minister are upon this footing they can mutually trust one another; but when the contrary is the case, it will always fare ill with one or other of them.

CHAPTER XVIII

Flatterers Should Be Shunned

One error into which Princes, unless very prudent or very fortunate in their choice of friends, are apt to fall, is of so great importance that I must not pass it over. I mean in respect of flatterers. These abound in Courts, because men take such pleasure in their own concerns, and so deceive themselves with regard to them, that they can hardly escape this plague; while even in the effort to escape it there is risk of their incurring contempt.

For there is no way to guard against flattery but by letting it be seen that you take no offense in hearing the truth: but when everyone is free to tell you the truth respect falls short. Wherefore a prudent Prince should follow a middle course, by choosing certain discreet men from among his subjects, and allowing them alone free leave to speak their minds on any matter on which he asks their opinion, and on none other. But he ought to ask their opinion on everything, and after hearing what they have to say, should reflect and judge for himself. And with these counselors collectively, and with each of them separately, his bearing should be such, that each and all of them may know that the more freely they declare their thoughts the better they will be liked. Besides these, the Prince should hearken to no others, but should follow the course determined on, and afterwards adhere firmly to his resolves. Whoever acts otherwise is either undone by flatterers, or from continually vacillating as opinions vary, comes to be held in light esteem.

A Prince ought always to take counsel, but at such times and reasons only as he himself pleases, and not when it pleases others; nay, he should discourage every one from obtruding advice on matters on which it is not sought. But he should be free in asking advice, and afterwards as regards the matters on which he has asked it, a patient hearer of the truth, and even displeased should he perceive that any one, from whatever motive, keeps it back.

But those who think that every Prince who has a name for prudence owes it to the wise counselors he has around him, and not to any merit of his own, are certainly mistaken; since it is an unerring rule and of universal application that a Prince who is not wise himself cannot be well advised by others, unless by chance he surrender himself to be wholly governed by some one adviser who happens to be supremely prudent; in which case he may, indeed, be well advised; but not for long, since such an adviser will soon deprive him of his Government. If he listen to a multitude of advisers, the Prince who is not wise will never have consistent counsels, nor will he know of himself how to reconcile them. Each of his counselors will study his own advantage, and the Prince will be unable to detect or correct them. Nor could it well be otherwise, for men will always grow rogues on your hands unless they find themselves under a necessity to be honest.

Hence it follows that good counsels, whenever they come, have their origin in the prudence of the Prince, and not the prudence of the Prince in wise counsels.

Chapter XIX

The Role of Fortune

I am not ignorant that many have been and are of the opinion that human affairs are so governed by Fortune and by God that men cannot alter them by any prudence of theirs, and indeed have no remedy against them, and for this reason have come to think that it is not worthwhile to labour much about anything, but that they must leave everything to be determined by chance.

Often when I turn the matter over, I am in part inclined to agree with this opinion, which has had readier acceptance in our own times from the great changes in things which we have seen and everyday see happen contrary to all human expectation. Nevertheless, that our freewill be not wholly set aside, I think it may be the case that Fortune is the mistress of one half our actions, and yet leaves the control of the other half, or a little less, to ourselves. And I would liken her to one of those wild torrents which, when angry, overflow the plains, sweep away trees and houses, and carry off soil from one bank to throw it down upon the other. Everyone flees before them, and yields to their fury without the least power to resist. And yet, though this be their nature, it does not follow that in seasons of fair weather men cannot, by constructing dams and barriers, take such precautions as will cause them when again in flood to pass off by some artificial channel, or at least prevent their course from being so uncontrolled and destructive. And so it is with Fortune, who displays her might where there is no organized strength to resist her, and directs her onset where she knows that there is neither barrier nor embankment to confine her.

I note that one day we see a Prince prospering and the next day overthrown, without detecting any change in his nature or character. This, I believe, comes chiefly from a cause already dwelt upon, namely, that a Prince who rests wholly on Fortune is ruined when she changes. Moreover, I believe that he will prosper most whose mode of acting best adapts itself to the character of the times; and conversely that he will be unprosperous with whose mode of acting the times do not accord. For we see that men in these matters which lead to the end that each has before him, namely, glory and wealth, proceed by different ways, one with caution, another

with impetuosity, one with violence, another with sub-
tlety, one with patience, another with its contrary; and
that by one or other of these different courses each may
succeed.

Again, of two who act cautiously, you shall find
that one attains his end, the other not, and that two
of different temperament, the one cautious, the other
impetuous, are equally successful. All which happens
from no other cause than that the character of the times
accords or does not accord with their methods of acting. And hence it comes, as I have already said, that two
operating differently arrive at the same result, and two
operating similarly, the one succeeds and the other not.
On this likewise depend the vicissitudes of Fortune.
For if to one who conducts himself with caution and
patience, time and circumstances are propitious, so that
his method of acting is good, he goes on prospering; but
if these change he is ruined, because he does not change
his method of acting.

For no man is found so prudent as to know how to
adapt himself to these changes, both because he cannot
deviate from the course to which nature inclines him,
and because, having always prospered while adhering to
one path, he cannot be persuaded that it would be well
for him to forsake it. And so when occasion requires
the cautious man to act impetuously, he cannot do so

and is undone: whereas, had he changed his nature with time and circumstances, his fortune would have been unchanged.

To be brief, I say that since Fortune changes and men stand fixed in their old ways, they are prosperous so long as there is congruity between them, and the reverse when there is not. Of this, however, I am well persuaded, that it is better to be impetuous than cautious. For Fortune to be kept under must be beaten and roughly handled; and we see that she suffers herself to be more readily mastered by those who so treat her than by those who are more timid in their approaches. And always she favors the young, because they are less scrupulous and fiercer, and command her with greater audacity.

Chapter XX

Aphorisms from *The Prince*

"One change always leaves a dovetail into which another will fit."

"Men are either to be kindly treated or utterly crushed since they can revenge lighter injuries but not graver.

"The wise man should always follow the roads that have been trodden by the great, and imitate those who have most excelled."

"Take aim much above the destined mark."

"He who is less beholden to Fortune has often in the end the better success."

"Those who come to the Princedom by virtuous paths acquire with difficulty but keep with ease."

"It should be borne in mind that the temper of the multitude is fickle, and that while it is easy to persuade them of a thing, it is hard to fix them in that persuasion."

"He who does not lay his foundations at first, may, if he be of great ability, succeed in laying them afterwards, though with inconvenience to the builder and risk to the building."

"A Prince can never secure himself against a disaffected people, their number being too great, while he may against a disaffected nobility, since their number is small."

"Men are always averse to enterprises that are attended with difficulty."

"Mercenaries and auxiliaries are at once useless and dangerous, and he who holds his State by means of mercenary troops can never be solidly or securely seated."

"A Prince ought never to allow his attention to be diverted from warlike pursuits, and should occupy himself with them even more in peace than in war."

"Many Republics and Princedoms have been imagined that were never seen or known to exist in reality."

"If we must choose between them, it is far safer to be feared than loved."

"If a man have good arms he will always have good allies."

"I do not believe that divisions purposely caused can ever lead to good."

"A Prince should show himself a patron of merit."

"The readiest conjecture we can form of the character and sagacity of a Prince is from seeing what sort of men he has about him."

"A Prince who is not wise himself cannot be well advised by others."

"A Prince who rests wholly on Fortune is ruined when she changes."

"It is better to be impetuous than cautious. Fortune suffers herself to be more readily mastered by those who so treat her than by those who are timid in their approaches."

About the Authors

Born in Florence in 1469, Niccolò Machiavelli was a widely travelled and deeply read diplomatic envoy for Italy's royal court. Also a politician, historian, philosopher, humanist, writer, playwright, and poet, he has been called the founder of modern political science for his efforts to arrive at a cause-and-effect formula for how to attain and hold power and conduct statecraft. Machiavelli's classic *The Prince* was posthumously published in 1532. It was made up of earlier papers and letters that he had prepared for his royal patrons. A short work of considerable innovation, *The Prince* is one of the most enduring and widely read pieces of Renaissance literature. Although the term "Machiavellian" came to refer to actions or people characterized by cunning ruthlessness, contemporary critics and scholars are taking fuller note of Machiavelli's ethics and reformist sympathies. The writer died in Florence at age 58 in 1527.

Mitch Horowitz is the PEN Award-winning author of books including *Occult America* and *The Miracle Club*. A writer-in-residence at the New York Public

Library and lecturer-in-residence at the University of Philosophical Research in Los Angeles, Mitch introduces and edits G&D Media's line of Condensed Classics and is the author of the Napoleon Hill Success Course series, including *The Miracle of a Definite Chief Aim* and *The Power of the Master Mind*. Visit him at MitchHorowitz.com.

CPSIA information can be obtained
at www.ICGtesting.com
Printed in the USA
JSHW032317271021
19919JS00008B/359